# EMERGENT FREEDOM

### A NEW
## BILL OF RIGHTS
### FOR OUR FUTURE

---

BY
DR. SHERIE GACHÉ

ISBN: 979-8-9871662-0-8 (Paperback)
ISBN: 979-8-9871662-1-5 (Hardback)
ISBN: 979-8-9871662-2-2 (Ebook)

www.drsheriegache.com

Publisher's Cataloging-in-Publication Data
Names: Gaché, Sherie, author.
Title: Emergent freedom : a new bill of rights for our future / by Dr. Sherie Gaché.
Description: First edition. | [Bostwick, Florida] : 44Freedoms Press, [2023]
Identifiers: ISBN: 979-8-9871662-0-8 (paperback) | 979-8-9871662-1-5 (hardback) | 979-8-9871662-2-2 (Ebook)
Subjects: LCSH: United States--Politics and government--2021- | United States. Constitution. 1st-10th Amendments. | Social change--United States. | Political science--United States--Philosophy. | Human rights--United States. | Liberty. | BISAC: POLITICAL SCIENCE / Human Rights. | PHILOSOPHY / Political. | SELF-HELP / Personal Growth / Happiness. | POLITICAL SCIENCE / Political Freedom.
Classification: LCC: JK275 | DDC: 320.973--dc21

*For our children's children*

# FOREWORD

---

*"All power is inherent in the people, and all free governments are founded on their authority and instituted for their peace, safety and happiness."*

—William Penn, (1677) 2<sup>nd</sup> Right,
*Pennsylvania State Constitution*


*Man is born free, but everywhere is in chains.*

—Jean-Jacques Rousseau (1762)


*I have a dream.*

—Martin Luther King, Jr. (1963)

# TABLE OF CONTENTS

# INTRODUCTION

Welcome to the Bill of Rights 2.0.

We the People live two lives of freedom. Freedom 1.0, the every day life you know now, and Freedom 2.0, the life we could live. This book can guide us to Freedom 2.0.

Without further distractions, flip forward into your Freedom 2.0.

Open to any page. You'll find at least one freedom you don't have. And then, you'll find many more.

Don't simply read this book. Use it to jumpstart your transformation into Freedom 2.0.

The world is ours to create. Begin by knowing, by finding the way. This book is a tool to show you how We the People can be free. Choose to advance toward freedom. Let's leave a legacy of freedom for the humans of the future.

Rights are about freedom, truth, integrity, and authenticity. These are not gifts granted by government; they are natural gifts from God/the universe. We declare them to protect ourselves, the people, from government or other institutional powers that may desire to remove these freedoms from us. We declare them to return to our sovereignty.

In a perfect world, no rights would be needed. Instead, we boldly declare our rights, because we live in an imperfect world.

The truth is that rights declared, verbally and in writing, have no power at all, if those in power show no reverence for these rights. Thus, it is up to the people to choose leaders whose first and foremost desire is to uphold rights as a guidepost, as priority interest. The breaching of any declared right should call for immediate removal of humans in leadership positions.

This declaration of written rights is a proposal, a blueprint for the future. The rights enumerated here include both established rights, revised for precision and potency, and new rights that urgently need to be established.

This guide provides a path to the implementation of these rights. Included are sub-rights, or rights within rights, that need distinct attention.

Within this book, previously declared rights are revised and often renamed for clarification to increase their potency. From the *Magna Carta* to the United States *Bill of Rights*, the initial declarations of our rights occurred during historical moments that did not allow for revision due to time constraints or neglect. This has led to clashes in meaning. Revisions strengthen declared rights and hopefully make it unnecessary to rely on the courts for clarification.

Rights must be supported by 1) the will of leaders and 2) established laws. Without these, rights have no value or application. *A declaration of a right alone does not get clean water to a thirsty person, stop enslavement, or save a human life.*

Of the rights that can be supported by laws, it is best to build consensus among international legal institutions, given that these rights are not national or regional needs, nor corporate or government needs, but instead human needs. Each country's government should prioritize the support of these rights.

# RIGHTS
# OVERVIEW

# FOUNDATION RIGHTS

## I. RIGHT TO ESTABLISH RIGHTS

*We the People declare the Right to Establish Rights.*
**Whereby** each human shall have the right to create rights.

## II. RIGHT TO BE HUMAN

*We the People declare the Right to Be Human.*
**Whereby** each Homo sapiens is equally of the human
species and thereby protected by rights,
and natural human beings
shall be protected as a species.

# BASIC LIFE RIGHTS

### III. RIGHT TO LIVE

*We the People declare the Right to Live.*
**Whereby** each human shall have the right to live, and
each human life shall be sacred.

### IV. RIGHT TO SUNLIGHT

*We the People declare the Right to Sunlight.*
**Whereby** each human shall have sunlight,
as necessary for life.

### V. RIGHT TO AIR

*We the People declare the Right to Air.*
**Whereby** each human shall have clean and free air,
as vital for life.

### VI. RIGHT TO WATER

*We the People declare the Right to Water.*
**Whereby** each human shall have adequate and clean water.

## VII. RIGHT TO FOOD

*We the People declare the Right to Food.*
**Whereby** each human shall have adequate
and safe natural heritage food.


## SUB-RIGHT: RIGHT TO
## NON-GENETICALLY-MODIFIED FOODS

**Whereby** *We the People declare the Right to
Non-genetically-modified Foods.*


## VIII. RIGHT TO SLEEP

*We the People declare the Right to Sleep.*
**Whereby** each human shall not be denied sleep,
as sleep is necessary for life.


## IX. RIGHT TO REPRODUCE

*We the People declare the Right to Reproduce.*
**Whereby** each human shall have
natural, reproductive choice.


## X. RIGHT TO SHELTER & HABITAT

*We the People declare the Right to Shelter.*
**Whereby** each human shall have shelter
from the weather and elements,
and a habitable space to live on Earth.

## XI. RIGHT TO GENETIC FREEDOM & BIODIVERSITY

*We the People declare the Right to Genetic Freedom and Biodiversity.*
**Whereby** all beings shall have sovereignty of their natural genes, to promote Earth biodiversity, and all beings shall have freedom from genetic modification.


## XII. RIGHT TO MOBILITY & MIGRATION

*We the People declare the Right to Mobility and Migration.*
**Whereby** all beings—human and other species— shall be free to move across Earth.


## XIII. RIGHTS OF EARTH

*We the People declare Earth Rights.*
**Whereby** respect of the utmost priority shall be given to the integrity of Earth, its oceans, lands, stone, core, and atmosphere.


*SUB-RIGHT: RIGHT TO RENEWABLE ENERGY*
**Whereby** *humans shall have the right to the most efficient, renewable energy sources available.*

# EXISTENTIAL RIGHTS

## XIV. RIGHT TO SECURITY

*We the People declare the Right to Security.*
**Whereby** each human's safety and security
shall be upheld and protected.

### SUB-RIGHT: RIGHT TO MILITIA
**Whereby** *We the People declare the Right to Form a Militia.*

### SUB-RIGHT: RIGHT TO BEAR ARMS
**Whereby** *We the People declare the Right to Bear Arms.*

### SUB-RIGHT: RIGHT TO SELF-DEFENSE
**Whereby** *We the People declare the Right to Self-Defense.*

### SUB-RIGHT: RIGHT TO JUST LAWS
**Whereby** *We the People declare the Right to Just Laws.*

## XV. RIGHT TO LIBERTY

*We the People declare the Right to Liberty.*
**Whereby** each human shall be free from enslavement.

# XVI. RIGHT TO SELF-DETERMINATION

*We the People declare the Right to Self-Determination.*
**Whereby** *all humans* shall have sovereign choice
and free will as to the beliefs and decisions of their own life.

## SUB-RIGHT: RIGHT TO PRIVACY
**Whereby** *We the People declare the Right to Privacy*

## SUB-RIGHT: RIGHT TO BELIEF CHOICE
**Whereby** *all humans shall have sovereignty over
their own belief choice.*

## SUB-RIGHT: RIGHT TO BODY SOVEREIGNTY
**Whereby** *all humans shall have sovereignty over
their own bodies and over their care choices.*

## SUB-RIGHT: RIGHT TO SPOUSE CHOICE
**Whereby** *all humans shall have sovereignty over
their choice of spouse.*

# XVII. RIGHT TO RESPECT & DIGNITY

*We the People declare the Right to Respect and Dignity.*
**Whereby** all humans shall have the right
to be respected and have their dignity upheld.

## XVIII. RIGHT TO CITIZENS' GOVERNANCE

*We the People declare the Right to Citizens' Governance*
**Whereby** all humans shall be respected and served
by their government with dignity.

### SUB-RIGHT: RIGHT TO OPEN GOVERNANCE
**Whereby** *all citizens shall have the right to know their
government's operations and proceedings.*

### SUB-RIGHT: RIGHT TO PROTEST
**Whereby** *each human shall be able to join others
to assemble peaceably to express views and dissent.*

### SUB-RIGHT: RIGHT TO PETITION
**Whereby** *each human shall be able to join others
to petition requests to the government.*

## XIX. RIGHT TO COEXIST

*We the People declare the Right to Coexist.*
**Whereby** all humans and other beings shall exist
in proximity and share Earth.

## XX. RIGHT TO FAMILY

*We the People declare the Right to Family.*
**Whereby** no human shall be deprived of family
by any government or institution.

### *SUB-RIGHT: CHILDREN'S RIGHTS*
**Whereby** *each child shall have the basics*
*of care and protection.*

## XXI. RIGHT TO CONNECTIVITY

*We the People declare the Right to Connectivity.*
**Whereby** each human shall have access to the internet
or equivalent technology to allow connectedness.

### *SUB-RIGHT: RIGHT TO NAVIGATION MAPPING*
**Whereby** *each human shall have access to*
*location knowledge.*

## XXII. RIGHT TO EXPRESSION

*We the People declare the Right to Expression.*
**Whereby** all humans shall have the sovereign ability
to express themselves, whether by
speech, protest, prayer, song, music,
art, dance, sport, and so on.

### *SUB-RIGHT: RIGHT TO VOICE SOVEREIGNTY*
**Whereby** *all humans shall be sovereign*
*over their own voice.*

## XXIII. RIGHT TO KNOW

*We the People declare the Right to Know.*
**Whereby** each human shall have the right to know,
any knowledge that is possible to be known,
limited only by science or spirit,
in the utmost search for Truth.
**Whereby** no government shall suppress,
distort, or corrupt knowledge.

### *SUB-RIGHT: RIGHT TO LEARN*

**Whereby** *each human shall have the right to learn.*

### *SUB-RIGHT: RIGHT TO MEDIA FREEDOM*

**Whereby** *media shall strive for journalistic integrity,*
*while being free from*
*government coercion or interference.*

### *SUB-RIGHT: RIGHT TO KNOWLEDGE SHARING*

**Whereby** *each human shall have access to and be able*
*to share creations or inventions.*

## XXIV. RIGHT TO EVOLVE

*We the People declare the Right to Evolve.*
**Whereby** humans shall have the sovereign freedom
to grow, change, and evolve in
a natural and uninhibited manner.

## XXV. RIGHTS OF OTHER SPECIES

*We the People declare the Rights of Other Species.*
**Whereby** respect for the lives of all other beings who inhabit
Earth is given priority, whether the beings are animal, plant,
and so on, to the expansion thereof.

# PART 1

# FOUNDATION
# RIGHTS

We begin with the Foundation Rights. These two specific rights are necessary for the creation of further rights.

These rights give We the People the right to create new rights, revise established rights, and certify protection without discrimination for all human beings.

These two rights prepare a foundation upon which to build all our other rights. They also provide a solid location of consensus, of universal agreement, as a starting point for the expansion of all our other freedoms.

# I.
# RIGHT TO ESTABLISH
# RIGHTS

*We the People declare the Right to Establish Rights.*

**W**hereby a right is a quality of freedom, and people have the right to create a declared right as a means to participate in community progress.

A right is sacred and absolute. No government can overrule or ignore a right through its power or its law.

This right allows the declaration of rights, whereby people have the right to declare rights as supported by the Right to Self-Determination. To declare a right is the progression of freedoms and protections toward a better world.

The *declaration* of a right is the key to its power. However, there are limits to freedom. Limitations often occur in the form of other rights, because rights modify, interact, and support each other. Limitation occurs when government fails to uphold and protect rights.

The declaration of rights means human progress. We move forward. Every declaration of a new right is a step ahead in the name of progress. To allow decades or centuries to go by without declaring rights that need declaring, waiting for them to surface by themselves, is detrimental and hazardous to life itself. The invention and evolution of rights improves and protects our lives. We declare rights to return to our own sovereignty.

## THE PROCESS

Rights are declared when humans need them. Historically, this happens after a war or a change in the form of government from a need expressed by a group of people. New rights are often created by a large number of people after excessive strife.

Usually, people demand their rights, and rights have traditionally been created so that those in power do not infringe on the people's freedoms. The situation that typically breeds the declaration of new rights has been we the people versus them the government. The idea is to obligate governments to act, or not act, in certain ways. However, the government is made to serve the people, and thus, there really should not be any binary but instead a cohesive symbiotic relationship.

The declaration process, historically, was done by an elite group of government-related officials, such as the U.S. founding fathers, who wrote the rights behind closed doors. Often, only the needed rights of a moment in history have been written at one time, leaving an absence of protection.

To declare rights, creative thought must happen—thinking, dreaming, imagining. Only with sharp minds and creative thought, as well as public discussion and sometimes decades of debate, have humans come up with rights such as liberty, freedom of speech and press, religious freedom, and the right to property.

Historically, rights were often put into writing quickly, or copied from an existing rights document. Often, they were brief and vague, or too complex, mixing rights that should be declared separately. They were formalized quickly, while the committee and public interest was alive. Due to these time constraints and limited intentions, they were usually poorly written and never revised resulting in a loss of clarity. Their very existence had to be sold to some group of people, and this final step of rights marketing to achieve ratification or adoption became the priority. This is the only way the rights could make it into a formally-signed government document.

The painful process of establishing rights has been well-documented, whether it happened in 1789 or 1948. The process can be packed with contention, disagreement, and lengthy meetings drawn out over weeks, months, or years. *Bill of Rights* creator James Madison worked so hard to ratify this revolutionary document that his words were barely revised. Five of the seventeen amendments were removed, and only ten of the remaining twelve were approved by the states for the final version of the *Bill of Rights*. Madison's words were barely revised, resulting in a *Bill of Rights* that has created confusion, leading to the necessity of rights cases often being decided by the U.S. Supreme Court.

However, once declared, the wording of rights must be pristine. No one wants one's rights touched.

As of this writing in the 21st century, with the tool of internet connectivity and free dialogue, rights creation can come from grassroots endeavors, a collaborative action of thinking and awareness. Some would say we need standards, but who has the right to make that standard? People do. Every person. Many people can form a feeling and an idea. A single person can write a sentence, but many can polish those words.

## THE IMPLEMENTATION

The declaration must be followed by real rights protection. A focus on the implementation and enforcement of rights must be made a priority.

To be enforced, rights require laws and social norms. Some rights cannot be enforced by the law alone. Respect is an example. Social norms can be powerful rights-enforcers. The evolution of laws and social norms are intertwined when it comes to the enforcement of many rights. Additionally, non-governmental organizations help make sure that specific rights are upheld by government.

The Right to Establish Rights is supported by the Right to Self-Determination and the Right to Expression, two supporting rights found in the Existential Rights section.

# II.
# RIGHT TO BE HUMAN

*We the People declare the Right to Be Human.*

**W**hereby every being of the Homo sapiens species is equally human—regardless of race, ethnicity, nationality, gender—and thereby protected by rights.

**Whereby** no human shall be deprived of their right to be a natural human being.

**Whereby** We the People signifies all the people.

This right was inspired by the failure of the founders of the United States of America to extend the rights they had declared to all humans.

This right is also a necessity, in an era of artificial intelligence (AI), to prevent the destruction of the natural human being. Additionally, this right prevents the same potential consequences of human genetic modification and experimentation. Every human shall have the right to remain a natural human.

This right is foundational, because all rights may then be built upon this right.

# PART 2

## BASIC LIFE RIGHTS

All rights here must be priorities for all governments, institutions, and corporations. These eleven rights that ensure survival—life, sunlight, air, water, food, sleep, reproduction, shelter/habitat, genetic freedom and biodiversity, mobility and migration, and earth rights—fulfill the fundamental needs of the human species.

All of the basic life rights are more than just rights—each one is *a priority responsibility of leadership. Thus, these are priority rights*, as these are the basic rights that protect human survival.

# III.
# RIGHT TO LIVE

---

*We the People declare the Right to Live.*

**W**hereby each human shall have the Right to Live.
Each life is an individual and unique life, and all humans share an equal right to live.

Human spiritual belief systems support the sacredness of human life. Some common examples are as follows:

- In Christianity, the sacred book *The Bible*, begins with the creation of life: "God created humankind in his own image, in the image of God created he them." (Genesis 1:27)

- In Islam, protecting human life is the second of five basic necessities. Islam's sacred book *The Quran*: "And whosoever saves a life it is as though he had saved the lives of all mankind" (5:32).

- The Hindu belief upholds all life as sacred, because all creatures are manifestations of the Supreme Being. This is connected to the belief in reincarnation which is the repeated embodiment of souls in different species of life, all souls evolving and progressing toward union with God.

- The Buddhist teachings strive to end suffering, and the fourth step of the Noble Eightfold Path is "Right Action: not to destroy any life…"

- The Jewish religion supports the preservation of life with the concept of *pikuach nefesh*—a person must do everything in their power to save the life of another. Additionally, the Talmud states, "Whoever saves a single life is considered by scripture to have saved the whole world." (Sanhedrin37a)

- The Atheist worldview supports life with morality, reason, and science.

The Right to Live upholds every single, human life. This right forbids genocide.

# IV.
# RIGHT TO SUNLIGHT

*We the People declare the Right to Sunlight.*

Whereby each human shall have sunlight, a necessity of life.

No human shall be deprived of sunlight, as it supports the Right to Live.

Sunlight nurtures almost all living beings and warms one's spirit.

Sunlight also fosters the Right to Security, as the daily sunrise provides humans with a sense of human stability and renewal.

# V.

# RIGHT TO AIR

*We the People declare the Right to Air.*

Whereby all people shall have the Right to Air, oxygen being necessary for life.

**Whereby** air shall be protected, clean, and free to all beings.

With an expanding population, plus pollution and deforestation, the Right to Air is crucial to maintaining life in the future. As we protect and respect the Earth and bestow it with rights, we must protect and respect its atmosphere with the Right to Air. The Right to Air must be supported by laws that prevent toxic emissions by industry, such as sulfur dioxide, nitrogen oxides, and mercury. Our laws must safeguard air quality.

International law should contain baseline standards for the purity and safety of air. Local laws need to impose these guaranteed environmental standards on various industries. Cities with high levels of air toxicity should not exist. Toxic air is poisonous, affecting children and the elderly in the short term and all humanity in the long term.

All nations must make the Right to Air a global priority. Every country must have a Clean Air Act that limits toxic emissions, with no exceptions. Multiple clean air goals are inefficient and should be consolidated. The Right to Air is a survival right, a Right to Live supporting right. Therefore, it is not subject to debate by committees and forums.

Furthermore, the Right to Air guarantees that air shall remain free as a necessary substance for life, and forbids any action toward the privatization of air and profiteering by corporations. Thus, the Right to Air prevents conflict.

Air must remain free and safe for all.

As with all the basic life rights, the Right to Air is more than a right—it is *a priority responsibility*. We have an *obligation* to not pollute the air. To fulfill this life-sustaining responsibility requires drastic changes to society and industry. Air pollution of any kind should be stopped immediately. Additionally, deforestation—given that it affects air quality—is an infringement of our Right to Air.

This right belongs to all species.

The Right to Air supports the Right to Live.

# VI.
# RIGHT TO WATER

*We the People declare the Right to Water.*

W hereby clean water is necessary for life, water shall be considered sacred. As a basic life right, Earth's waters shall be respected and remain a free element, never disrespected nor owned.

The Right to Water shall not be infringed. Laws shall forbid industry to release toxins or otherwise pollute our waterways. Laws shall prioritize the protection of water distribution systems and forbid water abuse and mishandling of all kinds. Governments must be held accountable and responsible to uphold the Right to Water.

International law must search for better solutions to protect Earth's water. Regulation is needed, supported by local measures. One potential solution is to establish a global committee independent of all governments and corporations to regulate and ensure the Right to Water, with no single government having authority over its decisions. Water is a public resource and it must remain so. No one shall own it, and no one should establish a cost for it.

The following facts demonstrate how water is needed for survival.

- Ancient Greek philosopher Thales of Miletus declared water constituted the principle of all things.

- The human body is 60 percent water.

  The brain and heart both are 73 percent water, the lungs are 83 percent water, the kidneys are 79 percent water, and the bones are 31 percent water.

- Earth's surface is about 71 percent water (96.5 percent of this is saltwater ocean).

Three main issues define Earth's water problems:

- Less water is available due to overuse, water mining, and industrial pollution.

- Large, crowded cities may lack adequate distribution systems resulting in a lack of access to water for some people.

- Water and water distribution systems have been privatized without regard for human needs.

The overuse of water for agriculture is the world's main water problem. The majority of fresh water—70 percent—is used to irrigate crops.

Lack of access to clean drinking water is another problem. Unclean water may carry deadly diseases that kill millions of people globally. Toxic chemicals in water from agricultural runoff or factory waste—as well as waste from consumed pharmaceuticals and personal care products such as soaps, shampoos, cosmetics, etc.—can also be deadly. Recycled into tap water, these chemicals can affect health and reproduction.

Lack of proper water distribution has forced some humans to carry heavy water jugs for miles, infringing upon the Right to Body Sovereignty. Children who are forced to do this labor are having their Children's Rights infringed upon, rights found under the Right to Family.

Water habitats on Earth are insufficient. As a result of industrial pollution, and poor or outdated water distribution infrastructure, some corporations attempt to make water a for-profit commodity. Civilians are forced to pay for water, owned by the government or a corporation. Water may be transported in mass quantities by pipelines and supertankers, leading to absolute control of water distribution.

An example of water access abuse is transboundary water, or water that crosses state or national borders. If a river's water has its source in one country but flows into another, conflict may arise over which country controls the water. This situation can lead to an injustice and infringement of the Right to Water. Nations must put politics aside and enter into transboundary water management agreements that uphold the Right to Water and the Right to Security.

Abuse of our Earth's water may also happen when a large corporation buys permits to bottle water, paying private landowners or the government. The careless pumping of precious water from Earth for profit may deplete our natural water resources.

Over history, there has been a movement toward the Right to Water. As of the early 21st century, many countries had adopted laws regarding water, such as the U.S. Safe Drinking Water Act of 1974 (amended in 1986 and 1996).

This movement has been pushed by people at the local level, and then picked up by international organizations.

Here is a list of some 21$^{st}$ century water rights initiatives:

- 2000. Locals protested in Cochabamba, Bolivia over water privatization by a multinational consortium. The company was forced out by a legal settlement, but many people still lacked water in the region. In 2001, the citizens of five countries in the region wrote the *Cochabamba Declaration* codifying the Right to Water: "Water belongs to the earth and all species and is sacred to life."

- 2000. The European Union's *Water Framework Directive* declared water a heritage to be protected and defended, not a commercial product.

- 2002. South Africa produced a white paper on water services, titled "Water is Life, Sanitation is Dignity."

- 2003. The Third World Water Forum, organized by the World Water Council, presented a 60-page document titled, "Valuing Water for Better Governance." This paper was jointly published by representatives from industry and non-government organizations. The World Water Council has critics, however, due to its partnership with large corporations, whose real interests may be water control and privatization.

- 2005. The Economic Commission for Africa published "Water 4 Life," a report on a seminar that focused on water management in Africa.

- 2008. The World Health Organization (WHO) published the third edition of its *Guidelines for Drinking-Water Quality*, which established guidelines for local authorities to help them safeguard the water supply.

- 2009. At the Fifth World Water Forum, the president of the United Nations General Assembly spoke of water as a right, saying, "…water is a public trust, a common heritage of people and nature, and a fundamental human right." At this forum, the third edition of the *United Nations World Water Development Report* "Water in a Changing World," was published. This report is republished every three years.

- 2010. The Water for Food Institute was established at the University of Nebraska to conduct research and policy analysis on water use in agriculture and to improve the strategic use of water for food production on an international level. The institute searches for ways to produce more food with less water.

- 2010. Syracuse University in New York held a conference on the Right to Water.

- 2010. The *People's Agreement of Cochabamba* claims "the right to water as the source of life."

- 2010. The Friends of the Right to Water grew to include thirty-nine United Nations member countries joined in an informal voluntary association to promote the UN water agenda.

- 2011. The WHO published its fourth edition of the *Guidelines for Drinking-Water Quality*, to promote standards for sanitary water to prevent disease.
- 2019. The United Nations published *The Human Rights to Water and Sanitation in Practice*.

The Right to Water is also connected to the Right to Mobiity and Migration and the Right to Self-Determination, as the lack of access to water causes humans to migrate over Earth. The Rights of Earth protect the Right to Water, which ensures the Right to Security, the Right to Body Sovereignty, and the Right to Live.

# VII.
# RIGHT TO FOOD

*We the People declare the Right to Food.*

**W**hereby every human has the right to adequate, safe, and non-genetically-modified food.

The world has enough food for everyone, yet an estimated 800 million people live in hunger. Some countries estimate 65 percent or more of their people live in hunger. Countries need to focus attention on their resources to solve the hunger problem.

Several main issues define food problems:

- Climatic disasters such as drought, storms, floods, etc.
- Poverty
- War
- Government policies such as agricultural policy, high gas taxes, etc.
- Food waste
- Food contamination
- Genetically-modified food

The 1948 United Nations *Declaration of Human Rights* Article 25 states: "Everyone has the right to a standard of living adequate for the health and well-being of himself and of his family, including food."

The 1996 *Rome Declaration on World Food Security* set specific goals to reduce world hunger. The term "food security" means a population of people is more secure when people have adequate food. While individuals support their own alimentary needs, each government must be responsible for the food security of its people in extreme circumstances and during difficulties.

Governments must make the Right to Food a priority right. Governments and non-governmental organizations often work together to support the Right to Food. The United Nations has agencies that focus on food: the Food and Agriculture Organization (FAO), the World Food Program (WFP), and the World Health Organization (WHO). The U.S. government has the international Bureau of Food Security (BFS) within the United States Agency for International Development (USAID). In 2004, the United Nation's FAO created the *Voluntary Right to Food Guidelines* that offer Right to Food strategies and policy recommendations.

The Right to Food also means food should be safe to eat. The globalized food trade has increased international incidents of contaminated food and enabled the spread of infectious disease. In 1961, the United Nations' FAO established the Codex Alimentarius Commission, which meets annually to establish international food standards and to ensure fair trade practices.

The Right to Food upholds the Right to Respect and Dignity, for each human to be able to feed oneself in dignity. The Right to Food supports the Right to Live, the Right to Security, and the Right to Body Sovereignty. The Rights of Earth protect this right.

# SUB-RIGHT: RIGHT TO NON-GENETICALLY-MODIFIED FOOD

*We the People declare the Right to Non-Genetically-Modified Foods.*

**W**hereby all beings are protected against genetically-manipulated foods.

**Whereby** food is not contaminated by genetically-engineered food creations.

Genetically-modified (GM) foods and chemically-treated foods are not debatable as safe to eat. The safety level of these foods has shown to be toxic in test animals.

According to the *Encyclopedia of Toxicology*, the World Health Organization defines genetically-engineered organisms as those "in which the genetic material (DNA) has been altered in a way that does not occur naturally." While traditional agricultural practices have for centuries manipulated breeding or reproduction for desired traits, current technologies achieve more rapid and extreme results, such as crop resistance to insects and more rapid animal growth and milk production. The process is transgenic manipulation, which modifies the genome by insertion or removal of genetic material. Genetically-modified crops began in the mid-1990s, without safety testing.

This right supports the Right to Live and the Right to Body Sovereignty.

# VIII.
# RIGHT TO SLEEP

*We the People declare the Right to Sleep.*

**W**hereby no human shall be deprived of the Right to Sleep.

The Right to Sleep is a basic life right, because deprivation of sleep is an obstacle to a productive human life. Medical research documents the negative effects of lack of sleep on the human body. These include sensory impairment, poor brain performance, mood instability, heart problems, and weight gain.

Thus, this right protects each human from imposed sleep deprivation, whether by government, institution, or other entities, with exceptions only when such deprivation is necessary for survival and security, such as disaster or war.

The Right to Sleep supports the Right to Live and the Right to Body Sovereignty.

# IX.
# RIGHT TO REPRODUCE

*We the People declare the Right to Reproduce.*

**W**hereby each human has the right to reproduce.
To create offspring is a voluntary choice, as a human action that shall not be controlled by gender bias or government.

The population of the human species is growing in contrast to the dwindling numbers of plants and animals, many species of which are nearing extinction. Human overpopulation is reported to be a threat to *all* species, including humans. The United Nations estimates there will be 11.2 billion humans in 2100.

Future debates are likely—will overpopulation become a threat, and will humans implement a program of controlled population growth of their own species? Will humans choose to have fewer children without gender bias? The result of gender discrimination regarding offspring creates consequences, such as seen in China, India, and other countries.

The Right to Reproduce is a right supported by the Right to Self-Determination, the Right to Live, and the Right to Evolve.

# X.
# RIGHT TO SHELTER & HABITAT

---

*We the People declare the Right to Shelter and Habitat.*

**W**hereby each human shall have the Right to Shelter as a need of basic life.

**Whereby** other species shall have the Right to Habitat as a need of basic life.

Shelter or habitat is space to live, which enables a human or other being to thrive on the habitable or inhabitable terrain of Earth.

The qualities of shelter protect human life from dangers such as foul weather, violence, or disease. Shelter helps the physical body thrive while offering security, peace of mind, stability, rest, and a sense of dignity.

Shelter and human health are linked. Shelter allows a person to remain healthy and to function as a productive human being.

Other species also have the Right to Habitat. Without habitat, a species cannot find food or reproduce and is therefore forced to migrate or perish. This right of other species must be considered, respected, and enforced when any development by humans is planned. Natural resources must be shared and owned collectively between humans and other species to protect the natural food chain ecosystem.

The Right to Shelter and Habitat supports the Right to Biodiversity, the Right to Live, the Right to Security, and the Right to Respect and Dignity. The Rights of Earth protect this right.

# XI.
# RIGHT TO GENETIC FREEDOM & BIODIVERSITY

*We the People declare the Right to Genetic Freedom and Biodiversity.*

**W**hereby each human shall retain sovereignty over their personal DNA.

**Whereby** the genetic blueprint of all species shall remain sovereign to the being and shall not be tampered with, interfered with, nor imposed upon by human engineering.

**Whereby** natural selection allows a species to evolve, and this biodiversity protects against the homogenization of species.

**Whereby** natural seeds shall remain sovereign and not be owned or patented by governments, corporations, or institutions.

Genetic freedom is a basic life right of all beings. The ability for human and other species to retain natural, unaltered DNA, as well as the Earth's ability to retain heritage/natural/non-genetically-modified seeds, safeguards natural biodiversity and prevents the homogenization of any species.

No government, institution, corporation, or other entity shall modify, interfere with, or own the natural DNA of any species.

Protection of all species for their natural genetic survival must be a priority.

The Right to Genetic Freedom and Biodiversity upholds the Right to Live, the Right to Self-Determination, the Right to Habitat, the Right to Food, and the Right to Evolve.

# XII.
# RIGHT TO MOBILITY & MIGRATION

*We the People declare the Right to Mobility and Migration.*

**W**hereby all beings—human and other species—shall be free to move across Earth, and shall not be impeded by governments or institutions.

**Whereby** migrating peoples shall not infringe on the Right to Security of the inhabitants of any lands, thus preserving survival for all.

**Situations.** Four main conditions create the need or desire for migration:

- Poverty.
- Food or water shortages created by climate.
- Food or water shortages created by conflict or war.
- Persecution or the threat of enslavement.

International law supports the Right to Mobility and Migration. The 1948 United Nations *Declaration of Human Rights* Article 14, No. 1, states, "Everyone has the right to seek and to enjoy in other countries asylum from persecution." The 1951 *Geneva Refugee Convention* asserts that no refugee will be returned to a country where they face serious threats to their life or freedom.

Both humans and other species migrate for survival. Statistics show that millions of people are migrating on Earth at any given time. Additionally, millions of other species—animals, birds, fish, and insects—migrate annually across Earth, some seasonally, some territorially.

For humans, the Right to Mobility and Migration is challenging because it collides with others' Right to Security. Migrating people may be perceived as a burden on the receiving country and its citizens. However, migration is known to increase productivity, innovation, and biodiversity, so migration supports the Right to Genetic Freedom and Biodiversity.

Furthermore, the Rights of Earth must be preserved at the same time as the Right to Mobility and Migration. All lands must be protected from overpopulation and natural habitat destruction.

The Right to Mobility and Migration supports the Right to Self-determination, because any being may choose to protect its own survival. It also supports the Right to Live, the Right to Food, and the Right to Water. It is modified by the Right to Respect & Dignity, the Right to Security, and the Rights of Earth.

# XXIII.
# RIGHTS OF EARTH

*We the People declare the Rights of Earth.*

**W**hereby all the Earth, including sky, land, forests, rivers, oceans, substrata, and core shall be protected.

**Whereby** Earth's natural resources shall not be subjected to invasive chemical substances or genetic manipulation.

Earth shall be treated with respect for its finite natural resources, such that all actions affecting Earth shall take into consideration the best interest of Earth. The Rights of Earth protect against deforestation and habitat loss, human-caused soil erosion, degradation of water sources, loss of biodiversity, loss of air quality, and other resource depletion.

The countries of Ecuador and Bolivia initiated Rights of Earth. Ecuador's 2008 constitution was the first to include a declaration of the "Rights of Nature." Actions of protection under this law are "the right to an integral restoration" and the right to be free from "exploitation" and "harmful environmental consequences."

The *Universal Declaration of the Rights of Mother Earth* was created by Bolivia in 2010. This document describes Earth as a collective subject of public interest and a unique, indivisible, self-regulating community of interrelated beings that sustains, contains and reproduces all beings. It states that humans must achieve dynamic balance with the cycles and processes inherent in Mother Earth. Bolivian citizens may sue on behalf of "Mother Earth" for infringements upon its integrity. This law also includes the Right to Water and the Right to Air as two of its seven points.

Invasive chemicals polluting water lead to huge damage to ecosystems. Environmentalist Rachel Carson wrote in her book *Silent Spring* (1962):

> If the Bill of Rights contains no guarantee that a citizen shall be secure against lethal poisons distributed either by private individuals or by public officials, it is surely only because our forefathers, despite their considerable wisdom and foresight, could conceive of no such problem.

The Rights of Earth support numerous rights: the Right to Live, the Right to Water, the Right to Food, the Right to Air, the Right to Shelter and Habitat, and the Right to Genetic Freedom and Biodiversity.

# SUB-RIGHT:
# RIGHT TO RENEWABLE ENERGY

*We the People declare the Right to Renewable Energy.*

**W**hereby all humans have the right to utilize the most renewable energy sources to preserve Earth and support sustainability.

**Whereby** humans shall cease the depletion of Earth's resources by implementing the use of alternative renewable energies.

Earth's resources are finite and these limitations threaten life and habitat. Governments must provide infrastructure, organization, and financing to implement the use of renewable energies. Governments must work with corporations and citizens to find renewable energy strategies that do not have hidden sources of resource depletion.

The Right to Renewable Energy supports the Right to Live, the Right to Air, the Right to Shelter and Habitat, and the Right to Genetic Freedom and Biodiversity, as well as the Rights of Other Species.

# PART 3

## EXISTENTIAL RIGHTS

The existential rights are freedoms that are necessary for a quality existence but may not always be essential and necessary for basic survival. Therefore, we can survive without these rights, at a base level.

However, they provide us with a life existence that supports the pursuit of life, liberty, and happiness. With these rights, life quality is improved immensely. Each of us will thrive better with these rights, individually and in community.

# XIV.
# RIGHT TO SECURITY

*We the People declare the Right to Security.*

**W**hereby each human's safety and security shall be upheld and protected, prioritizing protection of every human life.

The Right to Security is an umbrella right, encompassing all forms of human protection, including physical tools such as arms and non-physical tools such as laws.

The Right to Security comprises two types of security—the individual *personal* security and the security of the *community*. Thus, the Right to Security applies to an individual's or group's need to feel safe and free from threat. The Right to Security could also be called the Right to Safety, as it fulfills a basic need to feel safe in body and peaceful in spirit.

Conditions that affect the Right to Security at the most extreme levels, such as war and conflict zones, climate disaster, disease, environmental degradation, migration, and government policies may infringe on humans' basic survival rights. To protect these basic needs, governments must create initiatives and just laws that prioritize protection.

When governments create laws to protect a human's Right to Security, they need to consider how these laws may infringe on humans' other rights.

The *Constitution of Pennsylvania* of 1776 stated the need for security: "WHEREAS all government ought to be instituted and supported for the security and protection of the community..."

The Right to Security is supported by eight basic life and survival rights that are necessary to feel physical and emotional security. These are the rights to food, water, shelter, sunlight, air, migration, reproduction, and sleep.

The Right to Security supports many rights: the Right to Live, the Right to Respect and Dignity, the Right to Body Sovereignty, the Right to Liberty, the Right to Self-Determination, the Right to Family, Children's Rights, and many more.

# SUB-RIGHT: RIGHT TO MILITIA

*We the People declare the Right to Militia.*

**W**hereby an organized, professional national militia exists to protect and defend its citizens, *to maintain a free and secure state.*

**Whereby** able-bodied citizens shall have the right to take up arms to defend a community on a local, state, or province level, if needed.

This right provides security to citizens at both the national and local level, protecting and defending people in a time of conflict or threat.

The Right to Coexist, the Right to Respect and Dignity, and the Right to Live are modifiers to the Right to Militia, aiding in the creation of a secure world.

# SUB-RIGHT:
# RIGHT TO BEAR ARMS

*We the People declare the Right to Bear Arms.*

W**hereby** each human has the right to keep defensive arms as protection tools for a necessary check against government tyranny.

**Whereby** each human has the right to keep arms and other protection tools in case of circumstances of survival and community protection.

The Right to Bear Arms is a sub-right to the Right to Security, whereby individuals shall have the right to own and carry guns, within the confines of fair and just law for the protection of all humans.

The Right to Bear Arms operates as a natural defense against government tyranny and takes a direct role in the protection of all rights.

This right is supported by the Right to Liberty and supports the Right to Live.

# SUB-RIGHT:
# RIGHT TO SELF-DEFENSE

*We the People declare the Right to Self-Defense.*

**W**hereby all humans have the right to defend themselves. The Right to Self-Defense derives from the *medieval* natural law, *Summa Theologica* (II-II, Qu. 64, Art.7), written by Thomas Aquinas in 1265. Aquinas wrote that harming or killing an assailant was justified as long as the defensive action was proportional to the assault, no excessive violence was used, and the killing was not intentional.

The Right to Self-Defense supports the Right to Body Sovereignty and the Right to Live.

# SUB-RIGHT:
# RIGHT TO JUST LAWS

*We the People declare the Right to Just Laws.*

Whereby individuals and communities shall be protected by just laws.

**Whereby** declared rights shall be protected by just laws.

**Whereby** no law shall overrule any natural right.

Each human shall be entitled to due process of law and trial by jury, as a procedure of just law.

No unreasonable searches or seizures are allowed, as a policy of just law.

In a perfect world, no laws would be needed—a world where people are good and respect others' wishes, assuming those wishes are wholesome. But in an imperfect world, just laws are necessary for communities' Right to Security.

How do rights differ from laws? Rights are innate and natural. Laws are constructed. Laws are tools to protect these natural rights and serve justice.

Laws protect humans, their rights, and their communities. Whether a right is protected by law or not is usually the decision of each nation's government. If a nation's laws does not provide sufficient protection, sometimes a state or city may step in to provide legal protection for a right. International law must be developed to protect all rights. When laws fail, sometimes non-governmental or non-profit organizations may step in to protect rights.

As Martin Luther King, Jr. wrote in 1963, "There are two types of laws: just and unjust... An unjust law is a man-made code that is out of harmony with the moral law."

In the future, laws shall expand to afford greater protection for humans' rights and the rights of more species.

The Right to Just Laws supports the Right to Coexist, the Right to Respect and Dignity, and the Right to Live.

# XV.
# RIGHT TO LIBERTY

*We the People declare the Right to Liberty.*

Whereby all humans shall be free from enslavement.
The defense and enforcement of this right must be priority.

This right has been declared many times. The following are recent documents that declare the protection of human liberty:

- The Thirteenth Amendment of the *U.S. Bill of Rights* (1865): "Neither slavery nor involuntary servitude... shall exist... "

- *The United Nations Declaration of Human Rights* (1948), Article 4: "No one shall be held in slavery or servitude; slavery and the slave trade shall be prohibited in all their forms."

- *The Cairo Declaration on Human Rights in Islam* (1990), Article 11: "(a) Human beings are born free, and no one has the right to enslave, humiliate, oppress or exploit them, and there can be no subjugation but to God the Most-High. (b) Colonialism of all types being one of the most evil forms of enslavement is totally prohibited."

The Right to Liberty supports the Right to Live, the Right to Respect and Dignity, and the Right to Evolve. In the future, this right shall extend liberty to all species.

# XVI.
# RIGHT TO
# SELF-DETERMINATION

*We the People declare the Right to Self-Determination.*

**W**hereby every human shall have sovereignty over one's free will choices, whether involving body, beliefs, or character.

**Whereby** the sovereign choices of individuals shall create no harm to others, nor infringe upon another individual's Right to Respect and Dignity and Right to Live, nor infringe upon group security.

**Whereby** any nation, religious group, race, or other human group shall have the right to exist, but shall not infringe on others' Right to Respect and Dignity and Right to Live.

The Right to Self-Determination bestows the ability to construct one's life with free will. All humans shall be free to be whomever they choose to be, regardless of social norms or constraints, so long as no harm is done and no life or property is destroyed, as stipulated by the Right to Live and the Right to Respect and Dignity.

The original meaning of self-determination may have originated in the colonial era, when governments held other regions as colonies. It signified the will of colonized people to retain their sovereign ability to determine their own future and destiny.

This right supports all rights pertaining to the sovereign choices of humans.

# SUB-RIGHT:
# RIGHT TO PRIVACY.

*We the People declare the Right to Privacy.*

**W**hereby each human shall have the right to their own privacy—of body, of biology, of home, of property, of family, of character, of action, of thought, of personal data.

This right is critically endangered—if not partially extinct—due to satellite mapping, internet data, corporate collection of databases, security checkpoints, and social media algorithms.

All humans shall retain the right to choose what information they share about themselves and how they share that information. Any action that contradicts these choices shall infringe upon one's rights to privacy and security.

No laws shall be created to infringe upon the Right to Privacy.

The Right to Privacy supports the Right to Security. This right is supported by the Right to Respect and Dignity.

# SUB-RIGHT:
# RIGHT TO BELIEF CHOICE

*We the People declare the Right to Belief Choice.*

**W**hereby all humans shall have sovereignty over their own belief choice.

The *Constitution of Pennsylvania* of July 15, 1776, Article IX, Section III, states the Right to Belief Choice with clarity: "That all men have a natural and indefeasible right to worship Almighty God according to the dictates of their own consciences."

The Right to Belief Choice often relates or interacts with other rights. The wise and civil use of this right will protect the Right to Respect and Dignity, the Right to Security, and the Right to Expression, including assembly, prayer, choice of clothing, and any action so long as no harm is caused to others.

The 1948 United Nations *Universal Declaration of Human Rights* declares, "Everyone has the right to freedom of thought, conscience and religion."

The Right to Belief Choice is supported by the Right to Respect and Dignity.

# SUB-RIGHT:
# RIGHT TO BODY SOVEREIGNTY

*We the People declare the Right to Body Sovereignty.*

**W**hereby every human shall have sovereignty over their own body, and this right shall not be infringed upon by governments, institutions, corporations, or social norms.

Every human shall govern the care of their own physical body. Every human shall retain the right to make all choices regarding their own body vessel, as their own property.

Technological birth modalities, such as options besides natural birth, shall not be forced upon any birth mother. Nor shall any birth mother be coerced to accept such options.

The Right to Body Sovereignty protects against body tyranny by governments, institutions, corporations, or others. This right demands laws, rules, and decisions that *value* the life of every human by facilitating optimum body-care choices without coercion, including:

- Protection against genetically-modified foods, toxic chemical products, and bio-engineered products and methods.

- Freedom from governmental or institutional invasion of one's physical body.

The Right to Body Sovereignty supports the Right to Live and the Right to Respect and Dignity.

# SUB-RIGHT:
# RIGHT TO CHOICE OF SPOUSE

*We the People declare the Right to Choice of Spouse.*

**W**hereby all humans shall have sovereignty over their choice of spouse and whether they consent to marriage, regardless of gender, economic level, ethnicity, race, or nationality.

This right protects the choice of all humans regarding whom they love and wish to marry.

This right protects individuals whose culture accepts or encourages arranged marriages to ensure they have the final right of consent.

The Right to Choice of Spouse supports the Right to Family.

# XVII.
# RIGHT TO RESPECT
# & DIGNITY

*We the People declare the Right to Respect and Dignity.*

**W**hereby all beings have the right to be respected and treated with dignity.

**Whereby** respect and dignity is an innate right of all beings, and no being has to earn, merit, or work to deserve respect.

Respect is a deliberate action. It is an active choice of conduct or behavior that each individual performs toward another. It is an act of will, supported by the Right to Self-Determination and uninfluenced by the recipient's conduct. Each person has natural dignity, and therefore, need not bow to social norms or group pressure to acquire respect. This right upholds consideration and appreciation toward every human, while celebrating the biodiversity of humanity.

The Right to Respect and Dignity shall also be extended toward other species and toward Earth.

The Right to Respect and Dignity supports the Right to Live, the Right to Body Sovereignty, the Right to Privacy, the Right to Genetic Freedom and Biodiversity and many others. It also limits the Right to Voice Sovereignty, when the spoken word harms another's dignity.

# XVIII.
# RIGHT TO CITIZENS'
# GOVERNANCE

*We the People declare the Right to Citizens' Governance.*

**W**hereby government is *for the people and by the people*—a leadership that respects and serves its citizens with dignity, integrity, transparency, and accountability.

**Whereby** government shall build a wholesome government and citizen coexistence to operate as a true and pure servant of the people, by pursuing the people's best interest for health and survival, prioritizing the support of all rights, and striving to eliminate a government/citizen binary separation.

**Whereby** government respects the people's *Constitution*, first and foremost, and any powers not granted to federal government are to be retained by the states.

**Whereby** all government servants are forbidden to engage in lobbying, patronage, influence peddling, and bribery of any form, so that the implementation of the rule of law and democratic values is priority.

**Whereby** all citizens shall have the right to vote, and interference of the voting process is forbidden.

**Whereby** public lands shall be protected and remain free from corporate or private use or interests.

People create the government. Therefore the government is a servant of the people.

The *Constitution of Pennsylvania,* Article 1, Section 2, titled "Political Powers", dated July 1776 and still intact, states this best:

> All power is inherent in the people, and all free governments are founded on their authority and instituted for their peace, safety and happiness. For the advancement of these ends they have at all times an inalienable and indefeasible right to alter, reform or abolish their government in such manner as they may think proper.

Precedent to this was the *Virginia Bill of Rights* dated June 1776, with a similar statement in Section 3.

# SUB-RIGHT:
# RIGHT TO OPEN GOVERNANCE

*We the People declare the Right to Open Governance.*

**W**hereby government is for the people and by the people, and when public servants perform its actions, these actions shall be public knowledge.

Informational limits or guarded knowledge, as exceptions to this transparency, shall occur only within the strategic aims of a well-regulated militia to protect the citizens' safety and promote security.

The Right to Open Governance demands a citizen-focused and service-oriented government that is open and transparent in its actions and decisions.

This right supports the Right to Citizens' Governance and the Right to Know.

# SUB-RIGHT:
# RIGHT TO PROTEST

*We the People declare Right to Protest.*

**W**hereby each human shall be free to assemble in protest, peacefully and without harm to life or destruction of property, and free from coercion by governments, institutions, or social norms.

To protest is an innate right through which humans may fight oppression and pursue freedom and evolution.

The *Constitution of Pennsylvania*, written July 15, 1776, precedent to the *Bill of Rights*, states this well:

> ...the people have a right to assemble together, to consult for their common good... to apply to the legislature for redress of grievances, by address, petition, or remonstrance.

The Right to Protest is supported by the Right to Expression, the Right to Self-Determination, the Right to Voice Sovereignty, and the Right to Respect and Dignity.

# SUB-RIGHT:
# RIGHT TO PETITION

*We the People declare Right to Petition.*

**W**hereby all people shall be free to present their grievances to their government, regarding policies that affect them or about which they feel strongly.

A petition is an expression against any government that may be breaching any of the rights herein.

For example, the writers of the 1776 U.S. *Declaration of Independence* listed over 30 grievances against the King of England.

The Right to Petition upholds the Right to Citizens' Governance and the Right to Respect and Dignity.

The Right to Petition is supported by the Right to Self-Determination, the Right to Voice Sovereignty, the Right to Protest, the Right to Respect & Dignity, and the Right to Security.

# XIX.
# RIGHT TO COEXIST

*We the People declare the Right to Coexist.*

**W**hereby all people shall coexist, regardless of belief, race, or ethnicity, in celebration of the biodiversity of humanity.

**Whereby** humans shall coexist and share Earth with all other species.

This right protects people and other species living side by side, in a world of different beliefs, races, ethnicities, and terrains.

Several types of coexistence are found within this right:

1. The Right to Belief Coexistence, which upholds the human-to-human ability to coexist peacefully regardless of spiritual or religious beliefs.

2. The Right to Racial and Ethnic Coexistence, which upholds the human-to-human ability to coexist peacefully regardless of race or ethnicity.

3. The Right to Species Coexistence, which upholds human-to-other-species ability to cohabitate geographically on Earth.

The ability to coexist has the power to abolish war. This right brings peace by shielding against conflicts, such as over land rights, water rights, resource governance, and self-determination in terms of government, and many others.

This right upholds the Right to Live and forbids genocide.

The Right to Coexist supports the Right to Self-Determination, the Right to Respect and Dignity, the Right to Live, the Right to Expression, the Right to Security, the Rights of Earth, and the Right to Genetic Freedom and Biodiversity.

# XX.
# RIGHT TO FAMILY

*We the People declare the Right to Family.*

**W**hereby no human shall be forcefully separated from family members by any government, institution, or other entity.

This right recognizes and protects the family unit as a fundamental, natural, social foundation of life. This right intends to supports this foundation by fostering every individual's sense of safety, belonging, identity, personal growth and progress, as well as the expression of self.

Under this right, countries have a priority obligation to foster the unification of families. The Right to Family is especially important to protect migrating people against actions that may separate families, through deportation or the detention of migrating people.

This right supports the Right to Security and Children's Rights.

# SUB-RIGHT:
# CHILDREN'S RIGHTS

*We the People declare Child Rights.*

**W**hereby all children shall be cared for and loved, as priority, and shall receive a name, a nationality, food, water, shelter, sleep, and health care.

**Whereby** a child's security is a priority; thus, slavery or exploitation shall be forbidden.

**Whereby** all children shall have access to learning and recreation.

Children's rights should be high priority rights for a future world. Every child's need for love, care, and security should be of the utmost concern.

This right is supported by the Right to Security, the Right to Live, the Right to Food, the Right to Water, the Right to Shelter, the Right to Sleep, the Right to Family, the Right to Liberty, the Right to Mobility and Migration, and the Right to Coexist.

# XXI.
# RIGHT TO CONNECTIVITY

*We the People declare the Right to Connectivity.*

**W**hereby each human shall have access to the global infrastructure that enables technological connection, and this connection shall not be infringed upon by government or corporations.

**Whereby** no government or corporation shall weaponize the means of technological connection, satellites or any other infrastructure, nor use these as instruments of tyranny.

This right supports the human need to connect with other humans, and fosters sharing, nurtures a sense of belonging, and provides knowledge which can foster human survival.

The Right to Connectivity supports the Right to Self-Determination, the Right to Know, the Right to Liberty, and the Right to Live.

# SUB-RIGHT:
# RIGHT TO NAVIGATION MAPPING

*We the People declare the Right to Navigation Mapping.*

**W**hereby each human shall have the right to navigational location information, whether provided by satellite or other sources, and this shall not be infringed upon by governments or corporations.

All humans have the right to know their geo-location and access global mapping, so they can move securely through geographical space.

This right is supported by the Right to Mobility and Migration and the Right to Know, and upholds the Right to Security and the Right to Live.

# XXII.
# RIGHT TO EXPRESSION

*We the People declare the Right to Expression.*

**W**hereby all humans shall have the right to express themselves freely.

Expression comes in many forms. This right allows all humans to be respected in their freedom to speak and their freedom to protest, as well as the right to pray, worship, opine, and express themselves in a variety of ways.

The First Amendment of the *U.S. Constitution's Bill of Rights* of 1791 lists several rights of expression in a single Amendment. For clarity, the rights in the First Amendment—religious freedom (belief choice), freedom of speech (voice sovereignty), freedom of the press (media), the right to assemble (protest), and the right to petition—have been separated in this document. Each has become its own sovereign right.

# SUB-RIGHT:
# RIGHT TO VOICE SOVEREIGNTY

*We the People declare the Right to Voice Sovereignty.*

**W**hereby all humans shall be sovereign over their own voice and their choice to speak or remain silent.

**Whereby** no government, corporation, or other institution shall regulate speech or deprive any individual of the right to speak.

**Whereby** only the people themselves shall govern the norms of their speech, promoting respect and dignity of others.

Each person shall be able to speak freely, with the ability to opine, in voice or in writing, without coercion, suppression, or regulation by governments, corporations, or other institutions. Each person shall also have the choice to remain silent.

This right is naturally limited by the Right to Respect and Dignity and the Right to Security, so that all people may live in peace and free of threats to their safety. Thus, *our words shall strive to be respectful and non-threatening, and confer on others respect and dignity, whether in agreement or disagreement, for a civil and blessed discourse.* We the People shall have the sovereignty to govern our own speech.

This right is supported by the Right to Expression and the Right to Citizens' Governance.

# XXIII.
# RIGHT TO KNOW

*We the People declare the Right to Know.*

**W**hereby each human shall be able to pursue knowledge, in the pursuit of truth.

We the People retain the Right to Know, whatever the knowledge pursued, constrained only by the evolutionary limitations of science and spirit, thereby fostering understanding of life and survival and leading to progress and evolution.

The Right to Know shall not be infringed upon by any government or institution in an attempt to direct people away from the known sources of truth.

This right is modified by public knowledge and private selves and is protected by the Right to Security, the Right to Privacy, and the Right to Respect and Dignity.

# SUB-RIGHT:
# RIGHT TO LEARN

*We the People declare the Right to Learn.*

**W**hereby each human shall have the right to pursue learning as a sovereign choice, to fulfill the natural human drive of curiosity.

This right protects the sovereignty of each human to choose how and what they learn.

Here is a brief timeline of learning:

- Ancient Greeks believed that education produced good citizens.

- The Renaissance humanism movement promoted each human's right to think and fostered the concept of education.

- During the Enlightenment period, the number of printed books increased, and people were inspired to pursue learning and knowledge.

- In the late 1800s, public education became an institution which formalized human learning.

The Right to Learn supports the Right to Know.

# SUB-RIGHT:
# RIGHT TO MEDIA FREEDOM

*We the People declare the Right to Media Freedom.*

**W**hereby all media shall be independent and free of all government influence, coercion, oppression, and political gain.

**Whereby** all media news sources shall take the oath of objective journalism, and media institutions shall serve We the People, to provide independent, factual news, both verbal and visual.

**Whereby** We the People's free voice shall not be regulated by information platforms or media, to infringe upon one's Right to Voice Sovereignty or one's Right to Self-Determination, pursuant to the Right to Respect and Dignity of all beings.

The original form of this right appears in the *U.S. Constitution Bill of Rights*, 1791, First Amendment, as "Freedom of the Press".

The Right to Media Freedom supports the Right to Voice Sovereignty, the Right to Know, and the Right to Learn.

# SUB-RIGHT:
# RIGHT TO KNOWLEDGE SHARING

*We the People declare the Right to Knowledge Sharing.*

Whereby the sharing of creations or inventions allows humanity to progress and evolve.

Humanity shall foster open and shared access to research, ideas, concepts, and inventions, for the pursuit of evolution.

Transparency of knowledge shall bring the generosity of progress and promote the advancement of humanity.

This right supports the Right to Evolve and the Right to Know.

# XXIV.
# RIGHT TO EVOLVE

---

*We the People declare the Right to Evolve.*

**W**hereby the human species shall have the right to pursue its natural evolutionary growth and expansion.

**Whereby** machine technology shall not infringe upon natural human evolution.

**Whereby** human life and societies may evolve new forms of governance.

**Whereby** the human species shall have the right to update rights as needed, to meet evolutionary needs.

Humans have the natural right to evolve. Evolution is a broad term of human-constructed meaning. New concepts may influence the evolution of humanity.

In science, for example, robotics, neurobiology, quantum physics, string theory, trans-humanism, and genetic engineering explore what it means to be human and non-human. In philosophy, it has been suggested that we may reconceptualize what "human" means in a "post-human" world and that humans are non-fixed, transformable, evolvable, and flexible.

Corporations attempt to profit from these new concepts, and governments attempt to militarize them. These attempts generate the necessity for a system of bioethics as humans evolve in the pursuit of a sustainable humanity and a cherished Earth.

This right supports the Right to Live, the Right to Genetic Freedom and Biodiversity, the Right to Respect and Dignity, the Right to Citizens' Governance, the Right to Establish Rights, and Rights of Earth.

# XXV.
# RIGHTS OF OTHER SPECIES

*We the People declare the Rights of Other Species.*

**W**hereby rights shall be extended to all species.
Human management and control of other species shall be reconsidered alongside the evolution of humanity, as all beings shall have the Right to Live, Right to Habitat, and Right to Liberty.

The coexistence between species must be protected, and humans must hold sacred the interconnection of diverse species. This interconnection fosters all life.

This right supports the Right to Live and the Right to Respect and Dignity and is supported by the Right to Coexist, the Right to Shelter and Habitat, and the Right to Citizens' Governance.

# PART 4

## CALL TO ACTION: BEING FREEDOM

This book shall make you aware of all the possibilities of freedom. You are ready to move ahead to Freedom 2.0.

Freedom is a lifestyle and a mindset. It's a way of life, ever-expanding without limitations. Our rights belong to us every single day—not just as a reaction to a historical event when oppression is heavy and felt.

Rights are a technology. They are *tools* that can improve the world.

There are 44 rights here, compared to the original 10 rights found in the 1791 *Bill of Rights*. This new expanded and restructured *Bill of Rights* is a blueprint for our future, our world of possibility.

Certain rights will appeal to you more than others. Which of the 44 freedoms are you drawn to the most? Get involved in these freedoms.

### Find out how to become freedom at
### www.44Freedoms.com.

Being freedom helps create a new world. As you go forward, you will see many things that you will question. Search for the answers and stay curious. Keep asking the questions. Some issues may call you to action. Speak up or stay silent—both are your choice. Stand solid.

Choose to be mindful where you put your energy. Pursue the things you want to learn.

Being freedom feels good. You know in your heart that this is the way humans were intended to live. Frustration and unhappiness disappear into the past as you advance into an unknown that you just know is right and good for all beings. You know. You are sure.

In what ways will you become freedom?

The Land of the Free welcomes those with courage. Tread upright and strong. Brush off any feelings of being overwhelmed. Every step you advance forward on this path will open up vibrant doorways for others to join, and change is imminent.

The evolution of humanity proceeds. With every right, many wounds begin to heal. Each person—whether focused on a single area or pursuing a broader mission—creates momentum towards a better future. Evolution is at hand, and We the People own the power to create a magnificent world here on Earth.

It's up to us to make all possibilities become reality. Become freedom. Own your freedom, fully and without compromise.

Spread the word.

Share this book.

May blessings come to all. May evolution beget our world on Earth. Forthwith.

WE THE PEOPLE
DO ORDAIN AND ESTABLISH
OUR EARTH
AS THE
LAND OF THE FREE.

# APPENDIX I

## GENERAL TIMELINE OF RIGHTS

- 4th century BC. Ancient Greece. Rights began as ideas of natural law, attributed to Aristotle and Heraclitus.

- 1215. Great Britain. The *Magna Carta* was the first official document outlining the specific rights of citizens, adopted after the Norman invasion of England. The barons forced British King John to sign the *Magna Carta* to reestablish former English laws. It outlined 37 specific rights of citizens.

- *1256-1274*. St Thomas Aquinas wrote extensively about the concept of natural law.

- The 14th to the 16th centuries. The humanist movement began in Italy and spread through Europe. The humanist thinkers of the Renaissance promoted the concept of the right to think and celebrated education and civic virtue.

- 1689. England. A bill of rights formally titled, *An Act Declaring the Rights and Liberties of the Subject and Settling the Succession of the Crown,* was written by the English Parliament, after the Glorious Revolution and the deposition of King James II.

- 1689. England. *Two Treatises of Government* by John Locke declared that under natural law, all people have the right to life, liberty, and property.

- The 17th and 18th centuries. Enlightenment philosophers focused on ideas, discussions, and books about freedom. The American and French revolutions in the 18th century put these ideas into effect with constitutional laws.

- 1789. France. The *Declaration of the Rights of the Man and of the Citizen*, was written in the third month of the 10-year French Revolution (1789-1799).

- 1791. United States. *The Bill of Rights* was written in 1789 after the U.S. Revolutionary War (1775-1783) but took two years to finalize and ratify.

- 1865. United States. The *U.S. Constitution*'s 13th Amendment abolishes slavery, after the U.S. Civil War.

- 1948. Switzerland. The United Nation's *Universal Declaration of Human Rights* was adopted after World War II.

- 1990. Egypt. The *Cairo Declaration on Human Rights in Islam* was written by Muslim countries, in response to the United Nations' *Universal Declaration of Human Rights*.

- 2014. South Sudan. The *Constitution of South Sudan* declared 26 rights after a civil war created this new country.

# ABOUT THE AUTHOR

**D**r. **Sherie Gach**é is an adjunct college professor, speaker, and consultant. Dr. Gaché has three graduate degrees, MS, MFA, and a special-awarded Interdisciplinary PhD in Communication and History. Her research focuses on exploring new ways to think about freedom. Her career path journey included nine careers. This expansive professional and life experience gives her a unique perspective on freedom and rights. Dr. Gaché has helped many global issues through non-profit organizations by means of educational service-learning. She has lived in the United States and Europe, in both city and country. She currently lives with her family in rural Florida by the St. Johns River. For collaborations, partnerships, consultations, and speaking, go to **www.drsheriegache.com**.

CPSIA information can be obtained
at www.ICGtesting.com
Printed in the USA
BVHW050318100123
655977BV00020B/283